Howard
Mingham

Waters of
the Night

Caparison

First published in 2012
Second impression 2013
by Caparison
imprint of *The Recusant*
www.therecusant.org.uk

Waters of the Night is also available as an ebook
as published by Caparison in 2010

Printed in Adobe Caslon Pro by
Printondemand-worldwide.com
9 Culley Court
Orton Southgate
Peterborough
PE2 6XD

Selected by David Kessel
Edited and typeset by Alan Morrison © 2013
Cover design © Caparison 2013

ISBN 978-0-9567544-8-6

Acknowledgements

Some of these poems previously appeared in *Hackney Writers' Workshop 1* (Centerprise Trust Ltd, 1977).

'Broken Water' appeared in *Orphans of Albion—Poetry of the British Underground* (Survivors' Press/ Sixties Press, 2008; second ed. 2010).

Caparison sincerely thanks David Kessel for collating Howard Mingham's surviving oeuvre and granting permission as executor of his estate for its publication; and Ken Worpole, for his thoughtful contribution.

Contents

In The Destructive Element Immerse

'It does not last long, this business,' Howard Mingham wrote in his poem 'Breath', suggesting a prescient acceptance or resignation. All of Howard's work struggled to reconcile itself to the diminishing hopes offered by a world that at times he found insufferable. Yet the man himself —who I got to know in the late 1970s and early 1980s, when he became a regular member of the Hackney Writers' Workshop—was not without an irrepressible sense of humour, mordant though it often was. He also genuinely enjoyed the company of other writers, and long hours of discussion and political debate. The poem, 'Darts', about a group of hapless darts players resident at *The Marion Arms* near London Fields, where 'now and again their arms, their darts and physics coincided', is both thoughtful and mischievously funny. 'They played as well as they could, No errors in their judgement, no judgement...'

Laconic observation was as much in his poetic gift as an anxious apprehension of a world that is frequently portrayed during or after rain or thunderstorm. The streets are empty, but temporarily, refreshed. This will not last for long. Memories or presentiments of some great flood seem to run through his work, and the fear of being submerged, and of drowning, are also ever-present. He was a poet of water, that destructive element which Conrad thought that we should all find ourselves immersed in at some point in our lives—not always to emerge again. Though Howard's work displays clear influences—from poets as various as Auden, Eliot, Dylan Thomas and Sylvia Plath—it is completely original in its declarative, occasionally song-like, register.

Had Howard lived, his would surely have become a vital voice in the world of contemporary poetry. The poem 'From Ward F5' ought to be in any anthology concerned with the agonies of mental and existential despair, where the romantic belief that self-expression might relieve the pain comes to naught. 'Poetry,' he wrote, 'has a different purpose: I shall adjust my aim.' Howard did not make a poetry out of despair, for as his friend and comrade David Kessel suggests, he formed and polished it against the grain of his affliction.

From time to time Howard and I clashed temperamentally, despite inhabiting the same geographical and political landscape, and I shall always regret that. In those days I was one of those who espoused the view that the world could be easily changed for the better, while Howard cast an unwavering gaze upon the ineluctable tragedy of the human condition— though he too had hoped for more, and remained politically committed until the end. I was devastated by news of his death, as were all those who knew him.

Howard Mingham was an intense, witty, and formidably talented poet whose untimely and shocking death robbed us of a special voice, as well as being a diffident but warm and engaging human presence. This inspired collection, thanks to the devoted work of Alan Morrison, only confirms the scale of our loss. It also creates a worthy memorial to someone who deserves to be remembered with gratitude, love and respect.

Ken Worpole, 2012

Tenderness And Renewal —
The Socialist Poetry of Howard Mingham

Poetry butters no parsnips. A fancy excrescence. At best, a mere condiment, a chutney? But poetry could have an inalienable personal and/or social motivational task; the making of substantive hope in desperate circumstances? Hence, the inescapable importance of the War Poets in twentieth century England. But what is this to a young schizophrenic, working-class lad in Hackney who took life and his politics so seriously, and wanted to share his sense of wonder at a process of personal renewal in the only way he was able, the written word. Also, his fury and concern at the dereliction of the lives of so many fellow Londoners, old and young.

Howard Mingham was born in 1952 in Norfolk and moved to Hackney at the age of ten. He had an elder sister and a younger brother. He was educated at Hackney Downs Comprehensive school until the age of fifteen, then after working at many and various jobs, he spent four years at Kingsway College of Further Education where, according to himself, he "failed again inconspicuously". I first met Howard, briefly, in 1976, when he was an inpatient in Hackney Hospital's notorious F Block (incidentally the location of one of the first, mental patients' union, Hackney Union of Mental Patients). I suppose he had drifted into a schizophrenic illness. I remember him as a tidy, modest, and thoughtful young man with a quiet sense of humour, but we hardly spoke. After this, he went to live at Arbours, a Laingian therapeutic community, where he achieved a good measure of "recovery" and learnt personal "growth" and "self discipline". Enough to be able to live alone in a Hackney Council flat, find a job, and make a relationship with a young woman. I don't know whether he was on any psychotropic medication?

A significant number of schizophrenics write poetry, maybe, causally or therapeutically. Probably, more "sensitive" individuals are both more likely to write creatively and to suffer mental illness. Indeed, writing poetry may be organically linked to the healing of schizophrenia; that abused and ill understood condition. Schizophrenia may be a diabetes of the mind caused by a traumatic disbelief. An existential—hormonal condition affecting mind/body coherence?

Futility is the emotional mark of serious mental illness and chronic poverty. It is painful to have insight into this — its character and origins. The "painful bits" are the useful living bits. Pain tells us that we are natural creatures, not illuded gods or fairies, but we are part and parcel of the natural world around us. Existential pain is the personal starting point of healing, of which poetry – naturalistic, metaphorical or ironic, can be an essential part. The struggle between the "deadly" and the "living" is at the individual and social heart of each and every person. Between the disunited, backward looking, hieratic or demotic vision, and the forward looking heart centred "democratic" one, a struggle which is maybe more acute in the schizophrenic, when the two maybe conflated or intertwined?

So a poem is the "clotted truth" of a personal-or political circumstance problem. A grammatical-emotive nexus. Only ruthless sincerity is necessary to write it; careful precise words, personal rhythms and objective assonance-

i

dissonance. Poetry is neither illusory or cerebral, indeed it maybe anti-in-tellectual, destroying illusion, centring in writer and reader in the solar and cardiac plexus (poetry is heartening work). A true poem acts as an affective template for personal growth, healing, transcendence. It confronts the deadly through affirmations, contradictions, discovery, astonishment with the life bearing threads and realities of ones own, and social existence. Hence the importance of the Survivors' Poetry movement.

I first got to know Howard well in 1980/81 at the Hackney Writers Workshop, which had met fortnightly at Centerprise since 1976. The alter-nate Wednesday meetings were convened by Ken Worpole and provided an opportunity for local writers to share their work with one another. Members read out short stories, pieces of autobiography, extracts from novels and poetry. We discussed our writings amongst ourselves and offered criticism and advice, also giving public readings and occasionally publishing our work.

Meeting Howard at the workshop, in a pub or in his spare tidy flat, I was struck by the simplicity, seriousness and warmth of his commitment to life and the people of the East End. A commitment which expressed itself in his painstakingly worked poems. His hatred of pretention, elitism and poeticism; and in his active membership of South Hackney Workers' Revolutionary Party. And his poetry, which he worked on for several hours daily, expressed itself in London rhythms: prosaic, dissonant, somewhat laconic; the forging of a prosody which allowed him to marry a personal lyricism with a pithy realism.

The chasm between labour and culture today is almost unbridgeable. This is deliberate on the Tory part and accepted as normal and alright by ordinary people. Working-class poetry is largely regarded as a social con-tradiction—oxymoronic. Poetry, which is the coming into consciousness of life, new life, the living thread which is inchoate, highly complex, both painful and wonderful, is regarded as a bourgeoise enclave. The inalien-able task of poetry to confront the despair and deadliness within existence and transform it in a matter of fact way into everyday and millennial hope. Good modern rock music e.g. The Clash, The Jam, The Free is the medium of most working-class poetry, particularly for youth, it's heartening work.

All true poetry is a poetry of survival; personal, social, national—the subjective intertwined with the objective. Working-class life, of which I know only a little, is an almost continual struggle for survival; meeting necessity with mutuality and dire economic difficulties with a commitment to shared struggle. Experiences, thoughts, struggle shared and the everyday pain of manual labour, of poverty and of others. Agape.

A witness of Kitchener's militaristic terror on the western front and in British colonies, Wilfred Owen (a man of humble background) consciously sacrificed his life to write his poems of fury and pity so that Britain and the world in general may survive this, all too human, deceit and carnage. ('Above all, I am not concerned with poetry. The subject is war and the pity of war'—Owen).

Historically, the British working-class movement needs to create a national popular *mythopoeia*[1] to carry it over into a proletarian-led society (similar to what Elizabethan writers did for a worldly Toryism four

---

[1] a narrative literary genre where a fictional mythology is created.

hundred years ago). Essentially, a new and altogether more democratic concept and practice of freedom. Popular science and mathematics would be the corner stones of this.

Poetry is both a metanoiac[2] and chthonic[3] discipline. Metanoiac, in that it is concerned with the inchoate, the emergent, the anxiety of the new, both of individuals and of society. The chthonic, in that what it feeds on, its substratum, is the underworld, the underground, the world of the emerging proletarian intellectuals.

Early one morning in 1984, Howard was found dead in the Cambridge Heath Road area of East London, having fallen from a block of flats. An 'open verdict' was recorded. The poems in this collection were originally published to accompany a reading and celebration of his poetry and life, which took place in November of the same year. Other poems, which first appeared in *Hackney Writers Workshop 1* (Centerprise Trust Ltd 1977), are also included. For my part, I wouldn't be surprised if Howard hadn't been 'bumped off' by agents of the secret state after an intense mind policing "suiciding" operation. They take the best of us, which makes a violent historical outcome almost inevitable.

A copy of Howard's note to me, 1983/4:

Dear David, I called round earlier today, and wondered if you cared to go to that do at Chats Palace or perhaps were already going. I'm not quite sure I'll be able to go myself but give us a ring and we can meet sometime anyway. I'd like to continue where we left of talking about God, Spirit, Soul, whatever. I think I was too hasty then. See you soon, Howard.

What poet worth her or his salt would not go through hell to write poems as tender and unsullied as 'After the Rain', and as pained and relevant as 'Broken Water'. I think Howard was a young man of historic significance; as poor, gifted, pure and dogged a person as the young early nineteenth century Millenarian, Joanna Southcott.

'The flower of fury, night.'
Alun Lewis

David Kessel
Whitechapel, 2012

[2] Carl Jung's term for the process of whereby the psyche melts itself down to then be reborn; 'psychotic breakdown'.
[3] Of the earth; earthy.

Waters *of* *the* Night

Howard Mingham

Confessional Poem

Hearts do not break.
They are torn and held
in pitiless fingers,
they are kneaded.

Now hearts are needed.

But what shock of joy.
What helpless blood
gushed happily.

Where now
from this butcher's shop?
In the street,
a puppy pulling.
There are cold cans
of cut horse.

There are bones, of course.

Hearts do not break.
If only hearts could break.

My own hatred dismays me.
They do not.
Devil, let us shake.

Sleepless Night

See the fox trot bent-pawed across the snow
And see, the sky oppresses him,
His tongue lolls, his back is low.

Through a long night emptily
And now the dawn and a morning hunger
Stretch, day-long, before him.

Fish

That fish knows everything.

Knows the weight of water,
how sharp air is.
Knows where the weeds are.
Knows what it did yesterday
and what it will do tomorrow,
eats accidents.

Doesn't know that Sunday follows Saturday.
Doesn't want to.

Is blowing bubbles
under the water still flapping.

Lighthouse

Your lighthouse winked at me;
I sailed for your rugged shore.

Your lighthouse winked at me;
I moved to your beaming smile.

Your lighthouse winked at me;
I moved closer still.

Your lighthouse winked at me
And I sailed at your boot-blacked rocks.

Your lighthouse winked at me
And your lighthouse walked away,
Quietly,
In socks.

The Cock

Sergeant among birds,
the cock raises the rabble.

He drills the sky with holes.

Failed blues-singer,
he practises.

Poor bird,
alone in the featherless morning,
snags the attention of strangers.

Old man
gargles.

He vomits out
the long
poisonous worm of light.

The Cat

Sleek in eye and fur
the cat, smoothly on the grass,
with purpose all its body knows,
lies soft with dead intent.

Envy-bright,
it watches solitary
the plenty birds.

Slowly he moves, rehearsing leaps,
mind certain as a cut diamond.

'Those things clutter the trees,'
said the Lord.

'I am in agreement,' he purred,
'And they remind me of Paradise.'

Complete in agreement
and altogether quick with life,
the cat, and ejaculation, leapt,
seized in a shriek the noisy clutter
and pleasing,
murdered it.

June

You may drown on a day like today
Or swim the dapple
Sink into the daylight eternally
Relish the apple

The green lane is a place, place
To unmoved, float
Where June with peaceful sisters
Draws summer to her throat

In the long baths lay
And bathe in the long, long day
I say
You could drown
On a day like today

Splash. The green rattles in the high
And the insect lives and the swallows dive
Bathe in the long long
Move to the sleepy
Song.

On Molwyn Bach

Shallow are the prints of any man
Who in this sullen heat
Clambers the rocks of this sheep-nibbled land
Seeking to plant his feet,
If only for a wind-bit minute stand
To see a piece of land not in rocked or brambled chaos
But in accidental beauty lie
And in that accidental range find friendliness.
But all the white sky with blank purpose
Hoist from green refection's pool
A squirm uneasiness.

Did ever soft lips hide such broken teeth
As the now scabbed earth's who leers with leprous grin
Showing all such sour delights as lurk beneath
And break to space to win the wind
To softness with an old whore's guile,
Shriek of gorse and hopeless, windswept smile.
And all the white sky with blank purpose watched
As the milkless earth
And the dry wind kissed.

Where the stuttering sheep by hunger led
And the stammering collie followed,
Here the mountain reared its head
And all its slow, green tears
Its cheekbones hollowed.
And high, the parched stones cracked with grief
As all the white sky with blank purpose
Out-stared belief and disbelief
And stared with blank purpose.

How the short mountain vainly reached
By ages bust and shorn and breached.
Here the hapless druid upward stretched
As in silence's furnace do the sapless trees,
Where the squeezed river runs
And the clinging pilgrim breaks his knees
As all the white sky with blank purpose sees.

Here blood and wood and water beg sweet purpose.
Here hangs the bitter crow in empty stillness.
Here the druid's altar would not stand.
Here lies the careless skull picked brainless.
Here leans the woeful tree blown voiceless
And neither hope nor megalith here could stand
But all the white sky with blank purpose.

What the Thunder Meant

It vanished in a halo.
Early morning,
the sun clearing its throat,
birds shining like pebbles,

the stream that could know no resistance
but laughter, goes.

It is vanished in the flow.
Asleep,
its body of motives stirring in dreams,
sharp as the canyon's brink,

sight, looking into that great leap,
opened and broke

silence,
snows collected in their drop,
night, and light on its toes
as every planet, balanced on the dawn,

and vanished in the morning smoke,
rolled a hand from the distance

and holding lorries to their convoy,
the distant cannon whispered and spoke.

Rain

We are raining, we are raining,
The roofs are sliding.
The sky rumbles, falls,
Machine-gunned to the street.

Inside churches
The candles stand weeping,
Burnt histories at their feet.
The time is melting, Lord,
It melts.

Inside, the shadows change
As faces by grey firelight.
Their bodies, coldly damp,
Shudder, as though touched by an elderly hand.
It melts, Lord, the time
It melts.

Under the awning, wax-like the bodies,
Cool as youth,
Watch the rain and the tearful clock opposite.
Another five minutes
Another five minutes they'll give it.

We are raining, we are raining.
The day sings in the gutter,
Homeless, free,
Its ringing chains hang from heaven.
All history sings:
He who was the sky has now become the sea.
But on the pavement,
On the banks of the tarmac stream,
The goosefleshed passengers await
The relief,
The scheduled saviour of the dream.

And the roofs remain.
They are newly sullen.
The vain attempt drip drips
From eaves and drainpipes.
The townhall, an armadillo, yawns.

After the Rain

After the rain a holy
Pagan light fell from cloud
And struck the pavement slab,
In all the canyoned silence moved no crowd.

But in the stinking mist alone,
In the incense of the dying rain,
I stood on the brown-soaked stone
And I heard the song of the drain.

'I am the hope and the escape.
I am the tunnel to the drowning sea.
I am the gay merry and the dismal
And I am neither the light nor the way.

'Into me rolls the runaway penny;
To all things I am sanctuary.
I am their church, their catacomb, their nunnery
And I am neither the light nor the way.

By the trickling cave on the kerb I sat,
My head stone-heavy in my helpless hands
And in the sour valley of the stonefaced flats,
The drain sang to me and I dreamt

Of those distant, waiting lands
Where none made, no promise is broken
And the streams run clear to the honest sands
Where no man has stood and thus no lie been spoken.

'Yes, into me rolls the runaway penny
And longs the hopeless refugee.
I am catacomb and nunnery
And I am neither the light nor the way.

'I am merry in song and sing of the sea
And into me trickles the washed-out day.
And I drink of the hopeless refugee
And I am neither the light nor the way.'

The Garden

When he opened his gates
it was like opening jaws.
And when he entered —
softly, fearful of treason —
he became absorbed. In this empty garden
he sensed a large thing,
a carnivore.
But there were only bees and beetles.
And birds, sitting in the trees like princes.

Too large to scurry, and anyway
not bothered by any urgent, insect worry,
he stood,
lips like a trout's, gasping for words,
stupid
as all the garden stared
his words all blown away.

In all of the trees and the flowers,
there were no mirrors.
And all he could hear in the flower-spattered rockery
was a rush of water, more vivid than mirrors,
the smashing of images,
the white and giggling falls
of a stream too swift for reflections.
All he heard
was its wordless business
and its joyful, gulping mockery.

Tree

Tree shakes ghastly in the wind.
Earth holds his roots.
Tree walks not

walks not in boots across the park.

Waist-deep in the hug
of his mother, struggles
like a horse in the dark.

Tree rattles his bones in the dark.

Tree, tall, cut in half,
stands stout as a pillar,
like a cenotaph.

Tree untidy as a scream.

Tree gone wild in the scheme.
Tree twisting. Tree loath
and resenting

the bargain of growth.

Ode

'...it is a basic Marxist concept that being determines consciousness, that the objective realities of class struggle and national struggle determine our thoughts and feelings. But some of our comrades turn this upside down and maintain that everything should start from "love" ...these comrades are seeking a love transcending classes, love in the abstract and also freedom in the abstract, truth in the abstract, human nature in the abstract etc. This shows that they have been very deeply influenced by the bourgeoisie. They should thoroughly rid themselves of this influence and modestly study Marxism-Leninism'.

Mao Tse-Tung
speaking at the Yenan forum on literature and art
May 2nd 1942

I am in confusion,
not to say entwined:
I dare not move for fear
of being strangled, slowly, by
the wire of theories
binding volumes.
I am bundled, kidnapped,
bundled into the car
of the absolute truth, driven
like a nail
through the woundless night,
gathering speed in the mindless dark,
hurtling,
panicking like a comet,
anxious of my origins,
striking with panic the soundless air

rush, the muscular romantic,
head on to the brick wall
of the church or factory or mansion-house
where the ugly, thug and glutton
dine on ravaged virgins,
O, for the brick-built mansion-house
solid in the void.
Without direction, fearful of conclusion
and confused,

I am plankton
drifting like a truck-flattened ghost
blind on the waters of the night.
Waiting for the whale.

The whale of the masses is inspired to move.
Hunger whirrs like a U-boat's propeller
in the deep Atlantic night.

I am petrol on the puddle of night,
my little bourgeois night,
oil, the machinery's surplus,
the city's sump.
I am petrol on the puddle.
Food for thought only.

You say I must learn the workers' language.
You say it does not begin with love.
I do not know.
I had always thought it did,
My love.

I do not wish to construct
the empty box of form
nor bury the coffin
or the body of a poem
beneath dumb and lumpy tons.
I do not wish to see my child
smothered with love
nor breed a snob
only I want
that if he speaks
he does not drone the drone
of the great beehive
or whisper in the underground city.

I am petrol
in the puddle
in the gutter.
Engines cannot use me,
dogs refuse me,
over me idiots mutter.
I am spread as a rainbow
for some to consider.
I am neither guns nor butter.

Let my son
have my features
but not be like me:
washed up on beaches.
Let my son do daring things
and see beyond his reaches.
Let him not
be the thing which sits in cities.
Let him blaze like an angry Jesus
in the synagogue night.
Let him not be pretty.

Let him know his left from his right
and not hop the old polemics
of the absurdly just and logically right.
Let him not shift his feet like the unemployed
or march
march like those paranoid
of nothingness,
comets
with panic snapping at their tails.

Do not let him sing
the song of the bullet in the dark
but rather this song in the empty dark
than the snap and hapless bark
of the guardian of freedom.

Let him not glad
wave the mad flag
or crazy beat the drum.
Do not let him hang
limp as a flag on a hot day
when the new order has come.

Let him deny three times
before cock-crow,
let him love, deny
and know.
Let him know despair
at least once before he dies.
Let him know love,
its pretty lies,
let him sing the screams
and cry the cries.
Let him die many times.

Let my son rise
each day like a sun.
Do not let him bathe
In the washing-machine of revolution.
Let him turn restless in the night
and dream of solutions.
Let my son fight
in many revolutions
and wake to the day.

Let him rise each day
and modestly study
the large and airy body
of abstractions.

Thought in Mayola Street, Hackney

I think we must be in the time of plague
when full carts rumble through the streets.

We are in the streets where painted letters mark
in rough message the gutted house
and thin lamps like skinny sentries stand,
spill light and thin the dark
which deep as ages drowns the land,
eddied by the odd dog's bark.

In the dead streets one hears the wailing.
Dragooned, the sobbing feet of legions
tread the street and strand.
The last ships are sailing
and left like a sailor's woman
the scrawny, pregnant land.

I think we are in the time of flags
when well-oiled men ride horses
and the eager mob of starving
wave their happy rags.

I think we are in the time of turning
when the turned wheel rumbles
down the running streets.
I think we are in the time of burning
when the glittering dark on its rising tide
brings in the nameless fleets.

To Scholars and Ken Worpole

1.

I have stood on carpets soft as cats,
soundless, in pastel rooms.
I have stood by windows where the wind
rips trees leafless.

I have stood by mocked-up tombs
and watched the wandering heedless.
Studying tempestuous tedium.

All life is a moment found
in the right museum.

2.

I remember that
once I lingered, watching,
in Hackney Town, in battery slum,
a man blow glass from his mouth.
But me, old mate, unlearned yet
chew cud,
blow bubble gum.

There are those who think
a poem is but a pun.
And the poet slurs drunk
with moaning lung
wheezing his words
into an empty bottle of a morning.

But how the crazy
chisel grey stone and weep beneath the sullen suns
who crack the coded megalith
and blow all to sand and dust and moans.

3.

There are weeds and how
the eager gardener
pulls up Springtime by its roots,
making way for roses.

There are those who think
a poem is but a bun
found in garden cafés.
And as the classical statue poses
there are those who wait for the most correct
angle of the sun.

Some cause coincidence.

And there are those who think
the song is found
in the wreckage of the slum.

Kenneth, I shall not expound:
what you have looked for
you have no doubt found.

But there are mountains, canyons in the mind
where publishers never wandered nor critics ever climbed
and where only a seldom sun has ever shined.

4.

In general I have mumbled
of fortune's cooks
boiling cabbage in a kitchen
industry.

All that boils escapes from books
thus, books
do not look at me.

And hunger,
do not feed me.

Let the dry leaf drop
silently.

DHSS Poem

It is a very civil kind of service
that is done deliberately here;
the forms do not intend offence,
the voices are not severe

but here in the quiet, our time is bought,
unworked days absolved like crimes,
and if you truly haven't done a stroke,
they'll post you money, like a bribe.

He accepts, he has accepted it,
opens like an optimistic flower:
beneath this grim-lit sky of ours
the insect minutes and hours devour

'in a long hunger that knows
no final dignity but power:
and under the weight of waiting weeks,
I think the boldest question cowers.

'At these windows they are shocked to abstractions
by the smooth confusion that lurks in the glass;
sometimes, standing here, I think I see
but, surely, it is all too terrible to grasp.

'No people come here but us.
We shuffle one large number.
And it is no use hating us:
Our fingers may encumber

'but our minds are for the moment lost
and motives that we do not touch enwrap
we two in our efficient slumber
I do not know what it is that taps.'

Something taps, some clock
or customer is seeking to accuse
or is it our vast body,
shuffling in its queues.

Settling into stares, we wait,
Make a harsh glance at fist-proof glass.
A history is being written by clerks.
But time, noticed, will not simply pass.

Elegy for Dead Innocence

In the brittle wood I walked at sunset after rain
And beauty snapped at me like a guard dog.

We smell of cities in our lacquered boots
Or the cold steel of the plough.
We carry lunches, paintbox or things that shoot:
We are hated landlords now.

With empty hands I came in peace
And my silent story told.
She eyed me with her million eyes
And I turned cold

In the dim sunset I walked after rain
And dimly tried for a pact.
But beauty weeps in diamonds. Men weep in stony vain.
And trust like a log is split
By the stony axe.

'Come not here who shelter from the rain'

By the ploughed earth I trod, by the wounded earth
And beauty raked me like a harrow.
My dumb dirge I sang at a shadowed hearth
By rut of cart and barrow.

'Come not here who would deny
The labour of his birth'.

Beauty pours in plenty. Men squirt their precious sperm
And sing of joy in loud alarm.
On bed of earth gulls tug the innocuous worm.
Short are the screams and sinister
The long and tender calm.

'Come not here
Who bit the apple and would not see
The shreds of the murdered worm'.

Darts

They played the match away that night,
met in the 'Marion'
and left laughing, 'our team',
just happy or full of confidence, I couldn't tell.

For two hours they threw darts
and now and again their arms, their darts and physics coincided
in a pub beyond this yellow light,
outside the door, not here.

They might have been in Normandy,
drinking that foreign beer,
touching strangers' hard arms,
laughing as their darts dropped short.

They played as well as they could,
no errors in their judgment, no judgment.
As they came in they were grinning
and everyone thought they had won.

Let Us Leave Our Puzzle Behind Us

Plimsolls:
Shoes built in the canvas on the floor.
Such monuments as these we leave behind us.
And deserted bra.

We have laid these goodly hours beneath our heads
As white pillows on which we sighed.
We have exhausted the weakened, creaking bed
With a long night's ride.

And now the moonlight on our wrecked clothes.
All this sloughed skin of decorum
Should be left forever on a dried-out beach
Where birds do not visit and the sea does not reach
And against the day
Love does not button up tight.

Who would guess what lies beneath
The nylon and the suede?
Let us leave a dereliction behind us
And let them reconstruct our bodies
As they now do ancient forums.

Let us leave our puzzle to future minds
And let them solve it by what they touching find.

A Cup of Burnt Brazil

I. *The Dream*

The dust
stepped on a megaton of augusts

startles from its bracken bush
a bird-like shriek of disgusts —

a hundred miles of empty road
burning on the bonnet, plastic as a hawk's beak

a viper of oil-black water
insinuates its thin tongues from dump to tip

recoils at every touch of earth.
Full-faced with heat, numbed

pale with eternal sickness,
clutched on two twigs tied with bracken-string,

in a mirage, some half-human
staggers down to it bended knees

to drink. Still warm cities
howl in each destroying drop.

II. *The Money*

Black coffee, the cactus of our mornings
greens the deserts —

or stewed tea, straining the hunger
from boredom's belly;

lunchtime,
when the muscles return to the shoulder

and bread and chair equate. But steel
clarion of robots banging,

steel clarion that never tires
and returning

returning, returning to plough his greed,
slip in with a dancing threat, an ease

that grinds like sharp dust
into the eyes of the horrified, loan-strangled boss.

III. *The Poor Box*

He tried to smile
with gold sockets,

voltage bites his tongue —
he cannot escape it,

fouling his mouth
the colour of piss and

frothing with cheap laughter,
jokes tasting like copper,

he cuddles his sharp papers
in his priestly fist,

30

pretending authority, cushions himself
in the abuse of his silent office.

Every telephone
drills his soul with curses.

IV. *Lying on the Lumps of the Problem*

he jumps
from his five-storey window-block,

he hunts a holiday
in the cheapest ear he can hope to trust.

An unknown woman in the hot room
snores beside him for breakfast.

Eyes howling for the cops
who are heaving in their vestments,

a fear starves inside him,
clawing for breath.

He has that dream again.

V. *Da Capo*

He sleeps.
Fine.

Cards for All Occasions

When that worker's husband died
and she slipped beneath in a lake of loss,
I uttered blindly as we sat,
went home and wrote:

And I did not say, 'These things are not sent to try us.'
And I did not say, 'The universe is different but we are not.'
And I did not say, 'As the sum of our actions, our results remain.'
And I did not give those blessings of logic she would not
        understand.

She received black-edged cards,
flowers that somehow looked guilty,
elegant writing that leaned a little,
a message she would not recognise.

And I know she would give love
to an indifferent, mass-produced,
forty-two-pence-with-envelope card,
believing that like a child, it could do no wrong.

More than the sum of her actions,
she stares, drinking the thin tea of the vicarage,
held by something that persists, empties yet and gives
those cheap cards a love that worries itself past all understanding.

From Ward F5

I shall draw a glorious
and most mysterious picture of orange.
It shall be my long howl of despair
in face of the dawn.
It shall be round
and its centre hollow.
It shall be drawn so that when it is struck,
it shall sound as a drum.
And a red howl of agony
shall pour from it middle,
its soul.
It shall be incurable, this picture.
No doctor would dare come near it.
he would be engulfed
by its large and magnificent disease.
Nor dare any doctor come near me
armed with my pain and paintbrush,
I would present a fearful figure.
And colour him nine.

I am a pig
and pigs cannot draw.
I am a writer
and writers cannot draw.
I am impotent with pain and pen in hand
and a marvellous agony in my head.
My life is a beautiful wound.

They are trying to cure me
and do so by reviving the old
and long-dead, one time hopes
I have already had.
It is a joke,
but they are offering me
the freedom I have already tried.
They are trying to put me into contact
with other people of my kind,
to release me into another's arms.

They are trying to save the soul
I have already declared is not my own.
They are trying to give away
what I have already killed,
to re-sow the grain already milled.
They are trying to restore a talent
I have already worn out.
I am a writer
who cannot express himself
in anything but words.
This is his agony
and they are encouraging it.

I am calmer now
but the agony has not left.
I know already
all there is to know.
I cannot
for I have tried
and my life is one long essay.
I am an eternal attempt
at perfection.
I am a hundred darts
thrown at the bull's eye,
a thousand near-misses.
This is my agony:
I am the word
and the word has died
upon my lips
too many times.
Too many times for the pretence
to remain:
that expression relives the pain.   relieves?
Poetry has a different purpose:
I shall adjust my aim.

For She Still on the Ward

You lie there wretched
small
and the large concerns are heaped upon you.

Sometimes we wrap your head
in hot bandages
the usual, usual role.

It is all so much crepe
yet the concern is large
the business all
and your frame is small, small-boned
you are small.

One body in the meshed
machinery
stopped nothing.
When we are not in the well-oiled bolt
we are merely the small
unrhythmic jolt.

Broken Water

Dog-black-and-white it flits
skips in a gutter,
happy rubbish on the wind,
jerks in a gust, like traffic,
ducks and drakes across the city

past halls smelling of polish and parquet,
past halls smelling of cats and cabbage,
past tower-blocks and announced cement,
past dinner-houses of children scattered in play,
past the troops that do not work,
past the force that do not work,
past the idle

It ducks and drakes across the city,
dumb as rag
and blind where children are not pretty,
where roomfuls of family
do not burst from the curtained crevices,
where workless people remain unending
deaf and simple and uncomprehending
it ducks and drakes
past the hospitals
with the azure pictures of threatened lakes.

Beneath your feet an essence is running,
thick as oil, thick as drumming, an early
dark madness we had forgotten:
the sewers are swollen,
boxes and cardboard and cartons of water,
all that is used, unused, undone
kept by habits that tremble underground,
all effort to contain exhausted
are vomiting sound, vomiting sound.
All the parts are leaving,
clocks and daylight,
shops, factory, obedience, girls;

a bull of water swells,
boxes and cardboard and cartons of water,
wet symbols like bells
clatter in a flow of water and loss,
decay itself, removing us.

In these unused canals a flood,
derelictions that rattle on the light
and call to the body of your unemployed blood.
Where are the gifts
of the chain-department-store
and further, further there is more.

Behind you the pigeons cooing like pneumonia
and as always as hunger, unsteady cats.

Your small heart is cracking like bottles.

Not thought nor faith nor objects holds
in this broken water or arthritic catch.

Breath

It does not last long, this business,
our hard feet may drum
on the bald floor
but journey or dance it will not
sound on, outlast its moments
like the bell, still in the air
now and also dying, also dying,
tiring in the immortal silence.

Under a dry sun
our brevity bakes and cracks open,
dusty,
and our breath goes unnoticed
whether in, or out, or not.

And even in the soft grasses
where we writhe, watched by bulls,
in soft grasses we are a spasm

but among the thick waters of what
deep wilderness silent as glass
do we move muscle forward
so slowly, our weeping lost

and somehow breathe,
firm as fish,
permanent as loss.

If I Am But My Body

If I am but my body, then, buried,
Walk on the daisies on my grave:
Call me dead.
If I was but a spasm of life
Do not lay flowers at my feet nor marble at my head.

If I was but a gun
Then, old and obsolete, let me rust.
As triggers do, I did what I must:
And if I was death's powder or his lever,
I am now his dust.

I was harassed by empire, worried
By bugle duty.
I have seen wild horror
And his quiet carcass bounced in a cart
As though it were the cart's driver.

If I am flesh, then heave me into that deliberate cart
But if I am something like a whisper
Or the pump of your heart,
Then I was a flower,
Something of beauty. I am a river.

If, for the unknown purpose of pollen
I bloomed for a season
Or boomed like a storming tree
And settled my seeds even in the rotten,
Then there was reason in those silly flags,
Nobility in our mud-brown rags
And in me, humanity.
But if I was but my body, then bury and leave me forgotten.

Notes on Text

Idiomatic and stylistic liberties aside—as in the curious but detectably modernist uncapitalised 'augusts' in 'A Cup of Burnt Brazil', which one assumes alludes to the month(s), as opposed to a more abstracted use of the adjective — there is one amendment I felt was necessary to a line in the last stanza of 'Rain', which in manuscript form was written thus:

'The townhall, armadillo, yawns.'

[Note the conjoined 'townhall', which I have left intact as I suspect it was not a typo but a deliberate segueing of Mingham's]. My instinct has been to add in 'an' before 'armadillo', so as to emphasize what is presumably a faux simile, or metaphorical comparison; without any indication as to the presence of the word 'armadillo' after 'townhall', I found the line read a bit too obscurely. Equally, if the comma after 'townhall' was removed, it would still read rather obliquely, and seem more ambiguous, as Mingham might be referring either to the townhall itself or to someone who works there.

A.M.

An Eternal Attempt

It is a true honour to be in a position to publish the complete poetry of no doubt one of scores of poets who 'got away', before they had the time to make a lasting mark on the public page. Howard Mingham (1952-1984) is emphatically one such fugitive voice, whose obscurity thus far on the literary map is another classic example of the all-too-typical fate of the 'outsider' poet, undiscovered in his/her lifetime due to a perennial pattern of social and psychological struggle, and resulting exclusion from the mainstream of society (and thus from its literature). Poverty, too, plays an inescapable part in that fractured mosaic of circumstances that makes for the forestalled fortunes of every generation's obscured Judes.

In Mingham's case, schizophrenia further clouded but also magnified the intensity of his life and writing. It led him through the peripatetic hopscotch of psychical and literal itinerancy still so commonly endured by many schizophrenics to this day—a seemingly unbridgeable disjunct from the often relatively cramped parameters of what common 'reason' and 'rationality' define as *reality*. Yet in truth we all know deep down that 'reality' is an individually subjective phenomenon, infinitely filtered through the nuances of perception from person to person, and, in spite of humankind's efforts to distil it into a fount of shared experience through the melting-pot of *language,* ultimately exclusionary to the synthetic, estimated telepathies of empathic literatures, and the chalky semantic symbols we use to objectify and describe the inexpressible *thisness* of being, both animate and inanimate.

The inescapable likelihood is that there is an external reality into which one can tap (debatably through the melting screens of chemical disruptions in the brain, whether biologically autogenous, or narcotically induced), but entry means exit from self-hood, ego and identity. Debatably, those few who glimpse it, or are subsumed in it altogether, tend to be what psychiatry categorises as *schizophrenic*, or *psychotic*—shorthands for temporary or permanent experiences of *self*-transcendence, of the congealing of the ego, the de-fragmentation of personal identity, or, as the mescaline-assisted Aldous Huxley termed it in *Doors of Perception* (1954)[4], awareness of existence as a 'continually changing apocalypse'. An intense, vivid flavour of such brittle existential insight seeps through the plangent, broodingly beautiful, musical but troubled poetry of Howard Mingham, one of those 'psychical explorers' (*on whom* psychical explorations are *thrust* by combinations of circumstantial, genetic and chemical chance) to have found a means of communicating such incommunicable experience[5]. This gives Mingham's poems the feeling of inevitable events in themselves; of metaphysical epiphanies that impress an unsettling authenticity—and that there exist only 27 of them altogether, if anything, gives greater credence to that authenticity. One senses that each poem is a psychical piece of Mingham, not of his personality but of his essence; as if his was a deciduous inspiration, which stripped him psychically (and in that peculiar sense, reminds one of the impression left by Sylvia Plath's oeuvre; though while her's is *viscerally* metaphysical, or *muscularly* phantasmagorical,

---

[4] In its sequel, *Heaven and Hell* (1956), Huxley described the sensory experience of schizophrenia, his definition of the 'hellish' perception of 'reality' as one of 'lit-upness'.
[5] Past examples would include painters Richard Dadd and Vincent van Gogh, ballet genius Vaslav Nijinsky, and poets William Cowper, John Clare, Christopher Smart, Ivor Gurney, Dino Campana, Sylvia Plath, Nicholas Lafitte, to name only a handful.

Mingham's is more symphonic, hymnodic, lyrical (one might almost say Plath's was a more 'masculine' poetics). *Both* poetries, however, throw shadows of semi-disembodied, almost hallucinatory, consciousness. What we are left with in Mingham's 27 surviving poems, sparse in quantity but ripe in quality as they are, is not only poems, but ghosts.

It is ironic that material poverty is very often the bedfellow of a devastating intensity and richness of psychical insights, such as also funnels through schizophrenic consciousness; a combination of the two, then—not uncommon, since psychosis and privation are often inextricably linked—can prove explosive, both psychically and creatively. This was very much the case for Howard Mingham. His tragically short life wove itself through an ever-thinning social fabric stretched to its extremes during the very real apocalypse of Thatcher's disastrous 'Care in the Community' (a mass administrative hand-washing of the psychiatrically afflicted). Mingham was at times homeless, at others, sheltered in halfway houses. Literally, existentially and poetically, of *no-fixed-abode*. Historically, one thinks of such waifs and *poet maudits* as the Italian visionary poet Dino Campana, or hobo pioneer of 'singing poetry', Vachel Lindsay, or Welsh-born 'Super-Tramp', W.H. Davies, for examples of prototypes. All led vagrant, almost anchoritic lifestyles, wrote, and self-published, at great cost to their material wellbeing. Davies was fortunate to eventually be lifted by Arthur Adcock and Edward Thomas's sympathetic patronages out from itinerancy and into prolific literary fame; but Campana died in obscurity in an asylum, and Lindsay poisoned himself.

Mingham's own poetic pilgrimage was one undoubtedly dogged by the no less insidious social and political upheavals of the late Seventies and early Eighties, which impacted severely on the most vulnerable (most ruthlessly, on the mentally ill). But his brief literary life was touched in some meaningful measure by the admiration and support of an intimate circle of Hackney-based poets from similarly polarised backgrounds. He was also, crucially, nurtured and encouraged through the altruism of a community writing work-shop tutor, Ken Worpole (to whom Mingham dedicated one of his poems; p21). But Mingham's tragically premature death at only 32 meant his poetry was almost certain to be snagged on the barbed-wired barriers to 'recognised' literature (having not yet penetrated established territories), bounced back into obscurity, and denied the pot-shot at posterity many others of lesser ability have taken as par for the course. Though what we might call Mingham's 'Marxian Muse' was perhaps destined never to be taken up and 'patented' by the literary elites, if one subscribes to the Caudwellian[6] view—a dialectical materialist take on established literature—that poetic shape and content are determined by economic hegemonies; or, as Caudwell[6] put it more aphoristically in his *Illusion and Reality* (1937): 'Modern poetry is *capitalist* poetry'. It is hoped then that this belated collecting together of his small but important body of work will intercept that unfruitful trajectory and act as a late but much-welcome twist in Mingham's story; going some way to consolidating posthumous recognition.

As touched on, Mingham's brief life followed the typical patchwork path associated with that of a schizophrenic: billeted from psychiatric home to hostel to halfway house throughout a short and rootless adulthood. It is, then, hardly surprising that poets positioned as precariously as Mingham,

---

[6] Christopher Caudwell, real name Christopher St. John Sprigg (1907–1937), a Marxist writer and polemicist who was killed in the Spanish Civil War.

and in such a societally turbulent time, would have felt dislocated from the influential literary circles of the day, which, even at the more integrated periods, can still seem impregnable to those on the outside. It is quite distressing to have it again brought to our attention—via the posthumous serendipity of loyally preserved work finding its way back into circulation through a chain of chance acquaintanceship—that only within the last three decades, a poet who was at least ten years into his development, who had produced already some exceptional poems, had only been published in locally circulated booklets as part of a small co-operative of socially marginalised poets writing on the fringes of 70s/80s London society. Whether Mingham might have eventually become better known in time, had he survived beyond his early thirties, is impossible to know. Had organisations such as Survivors' Poetry existed in his day, Mingham might have found a more lasting print-life, as has his surviving friend, David Kessel (although, thanks to the latter's loyal preservation of his work, this writer, as assisting editor, was able to recommend the inclusion of 'Broken Water' in the posthumous section of *Orphans of Albion—Poetry of the British Underground*[7], thus securing Mingham's representation in a germane anthologized context). But the example of Mingham's socially and poetically obscure life should ring alarm bells through the halls of today's literary networks: that in times of recent past, so conceivably in times present, some genuinely gifted voices escape our notice, often simply by dint of deprived backgrounds, mental health problems, or a combination of both, inextricably linked as they often are.

Capitalism, upholstered as it is with material inequalities, has had much to answer for in the plethora of such invisible lineages of uncultivated talent, hampered by trappings of class and circumstance. It is not simply sad, but pathetic, that even today, society's puppeteers—MPs, 'tsars', media moguls, publishers—continually boast of increased 'social mobility' while oppositely maintaining and promoting a chronically *anti*-meritocratic culture where the mouldable mediocre is commercially prized over the authentic; a culture still riven by vast gaps in education and opportunity; one, further, only marginally shaken up since the tacit caste-system that devastated the scholastic ambitions of Thomas Hardy's autodidact stonemason, Jude Fawley (*Jude the Obscure*, 1895), fictional motif for whole generations of neglected working-class talents. Only three years before that prescient masterpiece was published, a 36-year-old ex-miner, and autodidact, James Keir Hardie, was elected as MP for West Ham, becoming the first working-class representative in Parliament. In 1906, Hardie was chosen as first leader of the newly formed Labour Party, and a further 29 Labour members were elected to parliament the same year. This unprecedented trouncing of a Calvinistic class system signalled the turning of the tide in British society. Eight years later, Robert Tressell's *The Ragged Trousered Philanthropists* was published, to small appreciation; but its revival and meteoric rise in popularity via circulation among British troops during the Second World War was thought by many to have contributed to Labour's landslide election victory in 1945.

Six seismic years of socialist transformation reshaped the British political map for the next three decades, shifting the tectonic plates of centuries-old heredities and hegemonies and consolidating a post-war consensus of common purpose (a crystallisation, in a sense, of the fragments of fraternity nascent in the nationally traumatic Blitz). That humanitarian reformation was

---

[7] Published by Survivors' Poetry and Sixties Press, 2008, ed. Barry Tebb.

truncated by Margaret Thatcher's materialistic mutant-strain of Smilesian[8] 'self-help' ("Victorian values"), turning the clock of social attitudes back a century, and, thereby, turning what should have been a lasting social enlightenment into what is now, retrospectively, a halcyon oasis of social progression. Today, under another Tory-led government, we are witnessing the final blows to the tattered vestiges of the Attlee Settlement: the privatisation of the NHS and the dismantling of the Welfare State with the wrecking-balls of grossly misinformed public 'opinion' (spoon-fed through Tory and red-top propaganda). But without those two bastions of our almost extinct 'social' democracy, countless numbers of us might not have even been alive today, such have been their incalculable importance in levelling up the laps, as far as politicians have allowed, of that most fundamental thing: longevity.

Unfortuitously, Mingham's poetic ripening progressed beyond the more compassionate dialectics of the Seventies, into the reverse dive of rampant materialism that has since branded the Eighties as a social dark age in the minds of many who remember them (and who are now witnessing their grotesque recrudescence in the brutalising mutant Thatcherism of 'austerity capitalism'). 1984 was a particularly loaded year: an Orwellian volte-face of industrial upheavals (the Miners' Strike) and privatisations of utilities—Thatcher's ruthless truncation of the Marxian trajectory of history. It was from such an atomised society that Mingham, a self-proclaimed 'Marxist-socialist' and no doubt politically shot-through by this point, apparently 'opted out', *permanently*. R.D. Laing theorised that schizophrenia was the rational resort of the over-sensitised mind to protect itself from *irrational* society; part of this process is an internalisation of those external anarchies and contradictions—and quite possibly Mingham, among many others, found this burden impossible to bear. Put figuratively, and to paraphrase Laurence Durrell, his 'brain's plumage' was turgescent with the grimes of congealed realities, like a pigeon trapped in a chimney, or a gull in an oil-slick. Without wings, did Mingham *choose* a more fundamental flight?

The tragic circumstance surrounding Mingham's death at only 32—he having apparently fallen, or jumped off the top of a tower-block—only goes to make one of his lines, on self-defenestration, 'he jumps/ from his five-storey window-block' ('A Cup of Burnt Brazil'), all the more chilling (one is also partly reminded of the suicide of American poet Hart Crane, who drowned after jumping from a boat, in 1932, three months short of his 33rd birthday). An 'open verdict' was recorded at the time, which adds a further mystique to Mingham's enigmatic poetry. In all aetiological respects, given his schizophrenic susceptibilities, hunted political convictions, and the eschatological motifs of his poetry, suicide is the most probable verdict. But suicide, as Al Alvarez conjectured in his sublime *The Savage God—A Study of Suicide* (1972), is a deeply complex phenomenon, the ideations and mechanics of which are peculiar to each individual. In terms of efficacy of *true* intent (i.e. the 'cry for help' quandary), 'suicide' is almost always, implicitly, its own 'open verdict'—a vague universal label for innumerably specific causes and circumstances; and sometimes, rather than being an attempt to 'kill one*self*', is more an attempt to 'kill' an *aspect* of oneself, or of one's life, that is felt to be chronically unsatisfactory to the point of being intolerable (and to which no readily apparent 'rational' solution is to hand, at least, not while 'the balance of the mind is disturbed', to echo an old adage). There is such a quandary as

---

[8] Samuel Smiles (1812-1904), Scots reformer, and author of *Self-Help* and *Thrift*.

to suicide not being so much an act of negation as one of ultimate affirmation of one's existence, or *will*—an impulse to somehow 'take control' of a feeling or situation in which one feels temporarily or permanently powerless[9]; albeit a stupefied affirmation scrambled into ultimate rejection of reality; or a phantastic self-reinvention through projected posterity. Mingham's was no doubt an ultimately unfathomable impulsion. Some clues might be excavated from the poetry itself. And 'excavated' is an apt term in the case of Mingham's eye for the transcendent in the carious—a kind of 'archaeology of souls'.

There is in Mingham's very eschatological poetry, personal fate, and schizophrenia, an uncanny echo of the equally gifted poet Nicholas Lafitte, who died at the even younger age of 27 (suicide). Like Lafitte—and in a kind of lineage from eighteenth century poets Clare, Smart and Cowper, all of whom were 'committed' at points in their lives, the latter two, diagnosed with *enthusiasme*, or 'grandiose-religious mania'—and in spite of having regarded himself an atheist, as in line with his conscious Marxism, Mingham's poems often resonate with what one can only describe as 'agnostic religiosity': a religious urge in one who, while ascribing intellectually to the apparent ineluctability of a post-Nietzschean 'godless universe', is psychologically and emotionally under-equipped to reconcile himself to such a spiritless reality. By 'under-equipped', this writer does not mean in terms of intellectual or poetic capabilities, but in terms of personality (and this has been a common-place chagrin for generations of poets; one which T.S. Eliot epitomised in *The Waste Land*, but himself ultimately overcame through his immersion in Anglo-Catholicism). This sensibility also lends Mingham's own conscious subscription to dialectical materialism a meta-textually salvific aspect: it is as if, perhaps unconsciously, his metaphorical landscape is constantly hankering towards some kind of metaphysical reconciliation, or salvation; and his ostensibly socialistic symbols and Marxian leitmotivs appear to carry along with them an atmosphere of almost chiliastic[10] mystique. Such a 'religious hunger', an appetite for spiritual nourishment, underscores Mingham's prosodic tendencies: some of his poems have a prayer-like rhythm, often punctuated with refrains, which emit a hypnotic, mantra-like quality.

Indeed, Mingham has a particular gift at the 'religious-sounding' aphorism; particularly beguiling, if not profound, is his tendency to subvert biblical proverbs: "Come not here/ Who bit the apple and would not see/ The shreds of the murdered worm' ('Elegy for Dead Innocence'); 'It melts, Lord, the time/ It melts' ('Rain'); and the sublime subversion of Christ's words in John 14:6: 'I am their church, their catacomb, their nunnery/ And I am neither the light nor the way' ('After the Rain'). Mingham's 'apocalyptic' poetry (a la Lafitte's), is perhaps a secular equivalent to the *enthusiasme* of the aforementioned eighteenth century poets; but it is *post*-Darwinian, so, soteriologically[11] dislocated: more what one might call 'atheistic anomie'. Of the same sort of existential neurasthenia as that which inspired the Victorian poet James ('Bysshe Vanolis') Thomson to pen his pessimistic epic *The City of Dreadful Night* (1874). It would seem both poets shared a petrified atheism —in a similar manner to Harold Monro's terror at 'no personal immortality'; more specifically, one which was in both cases reinforced by the dehumanising scale and 'dreadful' sights of their respective Londons, no doubt to each

---

[9] Perhaps the definitive study is Émile Durkheim's *Suicide* (1897).
[10] *chiliasm*: n. Christianity. The doctrine stating that Jesus will return, and reign on earth
[11] *Soteriology*: the doctrine of salvation (as in Christianity).

taking on aspects of colossi cramping their literary ambitions and smiting their tenacity with poverty and obscurity. Certainly ethical echoes of Victorian London reverberated in the capital of Thatcher's time, in which Mingham signatured the ultimate retort to Doctor Johnson's iconic topophilic trope[12]).

But whichever idiom one chooses, Mingham's 'poetic personality' is anything but that of the metaphysical acedia more typically associated with a 'Marxist' (Mingham was a lifelong member of the Workers' Revolutionary Party). According to David Kessel, Mingham was an atheist. But there is nevertheless the itch of a spiritual odyssey in his poetry, even if it is one ultimately dashed on the rocks of 'rational' resistance. Mingham's skepticism, though not *thanatotic*, is at best disappointedly apostate; and there's a doleful resignation in his evident feeling that if all is just as it seems and nothing more, then posterity is pointless in the absence of spiritual immortality. It's as if Mingham felt metaphysically anchored, oppressed, by his own Marxism, itself, perhaps, his conscious scientific attempt to rationalise an irrational, unpredictable cosmos, and the byzantine labyrinth of being. This inability to see a point to a purely ephemeral consciousness, something normally concurrent with a religious mind-set, seems integral to Mingham's Kierkegaardian[13] *angst*; he clearly finding no consolation in the ancient Stoic notion of the *mortal soul*, which perishes with the body. Mingham's sublime 'If I Am But My Body' captures this sense of futility in a spiritless existence, but defies its own will for oblivion in the minds of others through its sheer emotional force, almost an unconscious self-immortalisation (as in Christina Rossetti's haunting 'Remember', and Keith Douglas's 'Simplify Me When I'm Dead', on which Mingham's poem seems largely modelled). It's almost as if the apparent death-instinct, the tacit *suicidality*, is, as speculated profoundly by Al Alvarez in *The Savage God*, actually a will to *survive* death, to have a metaphysical clean slate; if you like, to metamorphose into spirit, so as not to die and enter oblivion, but to die, and then... start again; travel an alternative course of consciousness; repeat; or reattempt. As Mingham writes: 'I am an eternal attempt/at perfection' ('From Ward F5').

But arguably it is in this beautiful self-monody, possibly the most faultless and lingering of all Mingham's poems, that a powerful sense of past influence seeps in most noticeably, though one not easily pinned-down to a specific poem or poet. There's a similar tone to Keith Douglas's much-anthologised 'Simplify Me When I'm Dead'; but perhaps the closest cousin of Mingham's haunting lyric is that of the famous 'Anon' poem, 'Do Not Stand at my Grave and Weep', whose authorship has only recently been traced (though not conclusively) to one Mary Frye, an American, who possibly wrote the original around 1944 (I say 'original', because the poem has appeared in a series of subtle variations since its first publication; very much a poem readers felt somehow belonged to them, as expressed by impulses to add to and retune it over time): 'Do not stand at my grave and weep/ I am not there; I do not sleep./ ... Do not stand at my grave and cry, / I am not there; I did not die'. Certainly Mingham's poem bears a similarly ghostly resonance, as well as a fairly characteristic (of Mingham) allusion to war: 'Then there was reason in those silly flags,/ Nobility in our mud-brown rags/ And in me, humanity./ But if I was but my body, then bury and leave me forgotten'. But this is a

---

[12] 'When a man is tired of London he is tired of life'. *Topophilic*: strong, often morbid love of or attachment to a 'place', or one's 'home'; it also means 'homesickness' (*topophilia*).
[13] Søren Kierkegaard (1813–1855), Danish philosopher, author of *The Concept of Anxiety* (*Begrebet Angest*) (1844), *Fear and Trembling* (*Frygt og Bæven*) (1843), and other works.

distinctly affecting re-take on the recurring motif of self-mourning in British poetry—through Rossetti's 'Remember', Douglas's 'Simplify Me....' and Anon's 'Do Not Stand At My Grave...'; and, arguably, every bit as authentically felt and memorably signatured a mimetic work as Keats's early 'Imitation of Spenser', or even W.B. Yeats's 'The Song of Wandering Aengus' (arguably, a semi-imitation of Wordsworth's 'I Wandered Lonely As A Cloud': both share iambic tetrameter and similarly brooding rural imagery[14]). So even in a conscious jackdawing of past inspirations, Mingham still achieves his own distinctive take on the subject and structure chosen, and rises to the challenge with a masterful use of sprung rhythm: 'I was harassed by empire, worried/ By bugle duty./ I have seen wild horror/ And his quiet carcass bounced in a cart/ As though it were the cart's driver'. And what a brilliant motif for a poem, even if partly borrowed (but then aren't all of them?): that only a body which holds also a soul within it is worthy of commemoration (which, again, no doubt unconsciously on Mingham's part, taps into a spiritual, even Christian, sensibility). But my emphasis on a possible genealogy adumbrating Mingham's 'If I Am But My Body' is meant in no way to detract from the poem's distinct power and idiosyncratic tonality (though hopefully does detract from any perceptions of this Afterword being mere hagiography). Whatever the roots of this beguiling poem, it is arguably one of the truest contenders for a future anthology of fugitive classics that has come to light in decades.

Mingham's young age at time of death only goes to both emphasize the extraordinary powers he possessed at a still-maturing stage, and to suggest the seeds of promise for even greater poetry to come. What we are left with, however, and thanks to the loyal championing of his surviving friend and fellow Hackney poet, David Kessel, is a collection of work that defies any categorising in terms of 'schools', and constitutes its own strain of decaying beauty. There are only 27 poems by Mingham available for posterity, all collected here. But as David Kessel speculates, there may have been many more fugitive Mingham 'gems' that he himself never got to read, but which remain, for the moment at least, rumours and shadows.

What strikes one on first reading Mingham is his almost sage-like coining of original aphorism, his aslant descriptions, his clipped yet bristling tropes, his almost apocalyptic tone. One could argue that many of these aspects—together with an occasional 'knights-move' syntactical tendency, as in lines such as 'Let him not glad/ wave the mad flag/ or crazy beat the drum' and 'But how the crazy/ chisel grey stone and weep beneath the sullen suns', or conjoined terms such as 'goosefleshed' and 'stonefaced'[15]—are fairly typical of a certain form of 'schizophrenic poetry'; but then, that would be to affix labels, and to risk undermining (to all but Laingians) the threads of reasoning, in both subjective and objective material and metaphysical engagement. There is a detectable tension in Mingham's world-view between the sparring antitheses of—albeit subverted—spiritual insight and Marxist rumination. The latter manifests most starkly in the nature of the quote from Mao Tse-Tung at the beginning of the poem 'Ode', which essentially claims that any notions of class-transcending—therefore abstract—'love' are symptomatic of

---

[14] Although Yeats's poem has eight line stanzas consisting of slightly variable rhyme- and half-rhyme patterns, broadly ABABCDCD, whereas Wordsworth's has six line stanzas consisting of a strictly applied ABABCC rhyme-scheme.

[15] A kind of scrambled phrasing known as 'word-salad' which, for example, James Joyce applied more scientifically as a 'dream-language' in *Finnegans Wake* (1939).

a hampering 'bourgeois' influence on the minds of more 'bleeding-hearted' leftists; a Marxist dialectic which stigmatises Christianity and democratic socialism as sentimental distractions from the true proletarian cause. To a sensitive mind such as Mingham's, torn between the radical call for militant action and the strong heart-tug of pacifistic philanthropy, such gauche, hair-shirted proselytism is too simplistic, prickly, doctrinaire and misanthropic to be worn comfortably for long, if worn at all: 'I am in confusion,/ not to say entwined:/ I dare not move for fear/ of being strangled, slowly, by/ the wire of theories/ binding volumes.// of the absolute truth'. Again, in this Gethsemanean monody, Mingham draws on Christian imagery to help him express his terrible sense of ideological indecision, split between the spiritual and the political. His instinctive pacifism does not, however, inflect the wishes he has for an imagined offspring to triumph over the inertia of indecision: 'Let him not/ be the thing which sits in cities', he prays.

Whichever '-ism' Mingham *the man* bore conscious allegiance to, Mingham *the poet* comes across as a 'romantic' socialist, a self-confessed 'bleeding-heart' and bruised-tongued dreamer, thus one of Tse-Tung's *'embourgeoised delusionals'*, as he sardonically alludes to in 'Ode': 'I am petrol on the puddle of night,/ my little bourgeois night'. Mingham's voice is, before any partisan considerations, one of unpatented compassion; more socialist than revolutionary Marxist. And it is why, ultimately, he can only express his emotional confusion at a cause he had presumed to be based mostly in the heart: 'You say I must learn the workers' language./ You say it does not begin with love./ I do not know./ I had always thought it did...'. And here Mingham appears to be echoing Auden's hope for social transformation through a mass 'change of heart', rather than of uniform. If even a poet writing on the social and literary margins of his time was still ultimately constrained within a 'bourgeois' poetics through which to express his displacement—e.g. a *proto*-'proletarian' poet, the last stage before the fully ripened 'Communist poet', as according to Caudwellian dialectics[16]; or one of Empson's 'pastoral' proletarians[17] — Mingham was acutely conscious of such contradictions, and, as his poems demonstrate, preoccupied by them. Moreover, Mingham sourced these contradictions for poetic subject, ploughing their furrows songfully, as if for nourishment. This drive towards versified dialectic is part of what makes his poetry so fascinating.

In prosodic terms, Mingham tends to the free verse end of the spectrum, and skillfully sustains a series of longer poems in hybrid, sprung forms; yet his free verse has sculpted precision; any repetitions appear deliberate, carefully placed; any apparent technical lapses, superficial. Such forensic craftsmanship fits with David Kessel's own recollection that Mingham spent months working on a poem; and also accounts for his relatively small output. There is an urgency, an impulsion pulling this poetry, scented with necessity: it *had to be written*. Mingham skillfully sustains the longer poems, his compellingly dialectical style keeping one's attention through pieces that read effortlessly and fluidly, and feel shorter than they are. 'Broken Water' is one of the standouts: a Lewisian[18] miniature *Waste Land*[19], containing some luminous apho-

[16] see *Illusion and Reality*, Christopher Caudwell, 1937.

[17] see 'Proletarian Literature', *Some Versions of Pastoral*, William Empson, 1935.

[18] Alun Lewis (1915–1944), South Wales poet, author of *Raiders' Dawn and other poems* (1942) and *Ha! Ha! Among the Trumpets: Poems in Transit* (1945).

[19] There is a titular and thematic recapitulation of Eliot's 'V. What the Thunder Said' (*The Waste Land*) in Mingham's 'What the Thunder Meant'; the aphoristic style echoes Eliot's, but is still peculiarly Mingham's own; the poem closes, no doubt deliberately, just as the

risms and luscious tropes: 'In these unused canals a flood, derelictions that rattle on the light/ and call to the body of your unemployed blood'. Sublime.

But Mingham's transcendental qualities are no airy wisps, they are descriptive whispers, rich in image, aphorism and compelling leitmotifs; more khaki than bucolic—consumer society being, for the intensely sensitive, far from the ergonomic languor it is designed to be, but more of a daily psychic battlefield with lift-music. This metaphorical 'trench' mentality (or figurative 'fatigue-in-fatigues') accords with the conflicted consciousness of the schizophrenic. As Mingham's surviving friend, champion, and fellow Hackney-Whitechapel poet and schizophrenia-sufferer, David Kessel, frames it, Mingham's oeuvre has a psychically 'shell-shocked' quality. And Mingham was, as is demonstrable in many of his poems, strongly influenced by the poets of both World Wars—Wilfred Owen, Drummond Allison, Sidney Keyes, Keith Douglas, Ivor Gurney, Isaac Rosenberg and the brilliantly lyrical Anglo-Welsh poet Alun Lewis. To my mind, it is the latter three 'poet conscripts' of *verse khaki* who most noticeably adumbrate Mingham; above all Ivor Gurney, whose verse of anguished music powerfully foreshadows Mingham's similarly cadent psycho-poetics. There is, too, something of the *semiosis* sensibility of David Jones' *In Parenthesis* and *The Anathemata*[20] in Mingham's deeply symbolic poetry—although, in the latter's case, of an ostensibly *atheistic* (and humanistic) patina.

Mingham's sense of poetic comradeship and identification with the War poets[21] is perhaps not surprising for a poet himself at constant war with schizophrenia. It is a psychical association with the battlefield, allegorically grown through analogy with profound mental conflict. Army imagery even creeps into some of the less conflictive poems: 'Sergeant among birds,/ the cock raises the rabble' ('The Cock'); '...thin lamps like sentries stand', and 'Dragooned, the sobbing feet of legions' ('Thoughts in Mayola Street, Hackney'). It is a motif shared by other similarly afflicted poets, particularly those of socialist consciences; and one can picture Mingham being just the type of deeply empirical poet who, if he had been alive at the time, would have enlisted on an impulse of principle into the Republican side during the Spanish Civil War, as did John Cornford and Christopher Caudwell (the latter of whose aphoristic output Mingham's verse also bears some resemblance). This strain of *psychical khaki* is also apparent in the poetry of Mingham's surviving friend, David Kessel, whose own oeuvre (collected in *O the Windows of the Bookshop Must Be Broken*, Survivors' Press, 2006) draws much on the influence of poets such as Sidney Keyes, Drummond Allison, Alun Lewis and Keith Douglas. But as much as those recognised poets, Kessel cites Howard Mingham, his one-time friend, as chief among his influences. And this is indeed testament to the power of Mingham's poetry: it is writing that seriously inspires, that moves the spirit, and roils up one's own poetic sediment in response. No greater accolade could be given to a poet than that of inspiring his peers; though perhaps greater still, one who achieved this feat in only 27 poems.

Alan Morrison

'elucidation' promised by the title is about to sound: 'the distant cannon whispered and spoke' —though one might take this metaphor for mechanical destruction as its own answer.
[20] Both published by Faber in 1937 and 1952 respectively.
[21] Though Mingham's oeuvre also echoes some of the inter-war poets: the surreal lyricism of early W.H. Auden and David Gascoyne, and Bernard Spencer and Clifford Dyment.

also from
Caparison

Paperback poetry anthologies

The Robin Hood Book — Verse Versus Austerity (2012)
Emergency Verse — Poetry in Defence of the Welfare State (2011)

Poetry Ebooks

Arabesques of a Nervous Wandering by Alessandro Cusimano (2012)
Emperor Dragonfly by Sally Richards (2011)
Miracle & Mirage by Kevin Saving (2011)
Red Shift by Peter Branson (2010)

available to order at
www.therecusant.org.uk

to find out more about Caparison
imprint of *The Recusant* webzine
visit www.therecusant.org.uk